Gestational Surrogacy

A Primer

Victoria T. Ferrara, Esq.

Attorney Victoria T. Ferrara, Legal Director and Owner of Worldwide Surrogacy Specialists, LLC
2150 Post Road
Fairfield, CT 06824
203.255.9877
www.assistedreproductionlaw.com

The team at Worldwide Surrogacy:
Victoria T. Ferrara, Owner and Legal Director
Beth Anne Ferraro, Manager
Serena Lugo, Director of Surrogate Relations
Attorney Jeremy Hayden
Attorney Rani Clarkin
Jen McArthur, Social Worker/Case Manager
Erin Adams, Law School Graduate/Bar Admission Pending
Kim Goodrich, Paralegal
Dr. Michelle Loris, Psy.D., Ph.D. (Outside Consultant)

For more information on the Worldwide Surrogacy program, call the office at 203.255.9877, or email Attorney Ferrara at vferrara@victoriaferrara.com

ISBN-13:978-147925664
ISBN-10:1479265667

TABLE OF CONTENTS

1. Who Will Be Your Gestational Carrier

When Intended Parents decide that surrogacy is the process by which they wish to have a child, then the task of locating a suitable Gestational Carrier begins.

There are a number of ways that a Gestational Carrier may be found. One way is when the Intended Parents actually know someone who will be their Carrier. For example, in some cases, one of the Intended Parents may have a sister or friend who will be their Gestational Carrier.

While this may seem convenient and simpler in terms of having a woman available who is willing to carry a baby for a couple, there is something to be said for having a non-relative or non-friend as the Gestational Carrier.

Whenever there is a known or close-to-home Gestational Carrier, there are always more complicated social and family issues to grapple with. For example, if a sister becomes the Gestational Carrier and then birth mother for the child to be raised by her sister and her sister's Husband, or a brother and his partner, then who is the Gestational Carrier to the child? Obviously the Gestational Carrier is a relative or an Aunt to the child, but does her role become more significant to the point where it may cause discomfort or tension between and among the various parties.

There are some such cases that work beautifully but it is simply important to seriously consider all of the aspects of the relationships in order to insure a smooth and hopefully happy and positive surrogacy journey, as well as a happy, smooth and problem-free life with raising the child or children born as a result of the Gestational Surrogacy arrangement.

Although there is a greater cost or fee associated with securing a Gestational Carrier who is not known ahead of time by the Intended

Parents, such an "arms-length" manner of proceeding may present less tension and awkwardness in terms of going forward after a child is born. Generally, after a child is born, the Gestational Carrier returns to her life with her children, and her Husband (if she is married) and she does not have great expectations of keeping in touch with the Intended Parents or the child. Further, the Intended Parents have no obligation to keep in touch with the Gestational Carrier. In this way, they are able to maintain more privacy about the manner in which they brought their child into their lives. Most likely, friends and family know the child was born via surrogacy, however there is not a constant reminder at every family gathering where the relative Gestational Carrier may also be present.

There is no right or wrong way to locate or find a Gestational Carrier. Each surrogacy arrangement or journey will be different and it is important for Intended Parents to carefully consider all options and then follow a course that seems right for them.

If the path is to find a Gestational Carrier who is not already known to the Intended Parents, then the method of locating such a woman must be addressed. There are alternatives in following this path.

Intended Parents can attempt to find the Gestational Carrier themselves by going onto on-line forums or by placing ads online or in print media. Or they can use the services of a surrogacy agency, also known as a surrogacy matching agency, or surrogacy program. Either way, it is crucial to follow a screening protocol in order to make sure that the Gestational Carrier will be a medically and psychologically sound choice to become a Gestational Carrier.

A reputable agency will do the following screening:

1. Prior to proposing a Gestational Carrier to Intended Parents, her medical records from her pregnancies are obtained and they are reviewed and approved by a Reproductive Endocrinologist;

2. A background investigation is done;

3. A preliminary psychological evaluation is conducted; in some cases, a full psychological evaluation is done including the MMPI or PAI psychological testing protocol. Some agencies hold off on doing the testing since sometimes, the clinic where the Intended Parents plan to go for IVF treatment wish to manage the psychological testing aspect of the screening.

4. A social worker does an interview of the Gestational Carrier candidate in order

to ascertain facts about the candidate's lifestyle, habits and home life.

No matter how the Gestational Carrier is found, it is crucial that the screening is done thoroughly and carefully because clearly, the surrogacy journey is a journey that must be imbued with the most trust and confidence possible.

If the Intended Parents can afford to use the services of a an experienced and reputable surrogacy matching agency, this will be an important component to their endeavors. Surrounding themselves with a team of professionals who understand the nuances of the relationships that develop between the parties to the surrogacy journey, and who are familiar with the legal issues and necessary legal procedures, and most importantly, who make sure that a careful screening protocol is followed is of paramount importance to the success of the plan to have a child or children through surrogacy.

First of all the agency will locate the Gestational Carrier for the Intended Parents and propose the match to the Intended Parents. Then the team from the surrogacy matching agency will assist with the initial meeting and communications between the Intended Parents and the Gestational Carrier.

The team will facilitate appointment scheduling with the IVF clinic (fertility clinic) and will create a buffer when it comes to contract negotiations. It is usually better if the Intended Parents and the Gestational Carrier do not have to directly discuss compensation terms and other contract provisions as these discussions may be uncomfortable or even tense. With the matching agency team in place, this team can orchestrate and plan the contract drafting and legal counsel for the negotiations or contract review. Thereby, the money matters and other practical concerns in the contract can go through the lawyers as opposed to being discussed directly by the parties.

2. Choosing a Surrogacy Program (Matching Agency)

If you are going to work with a matching agency (an agency that will find a surrogate for you), look for an agency that will be there for you throughout the entire process, from finding the surrogate through the birth. An agency should not only locate your surrogate (also called a gestational carrier), but the agency should also help coordinate medical appointments, facilitate communication, organize travel plans, assist with escrow and money matters, and most importantly, plan and coordinate legal proceedings to establish legal parentage. Also, the agency should inform you as to the screening it conducts of its proposed carriers such as background investigations, medical screening and social analysis.

There are differing fee structures for surrogacy agencies. The fees are usually outlined in an initial document focused on anticipated expenses. The fees will most likely consist of the agency fees, ie what the agency charges to do the work it does, the fees for screening of the carrier such as psychological evaluations, background checks, and psychological testing. The fee outline may contain a range of compensation for the gestational carrier such as $20,000 to $30,000 depending on experience.

Gestational Carriers who have carried before for Intended Parents usually charge more than a first-time carrier. Additional fees that should be noted for consideration include: additional contractual fees for the carrier, legal fees, a reminder to investigate the fertility clinic's charges, insurance fees, if any, or a reminder that insurance premiums may be a consideration, escrow charges, possible travel expenses.

The agency should inform the Intended Parents who the representatives are of the agency that will work directly with them. For example, is there a case manager? Also, is there an attorney available to answer legal questions? Who is the main contact person? Is there a supervisory person in charge who can also attend to questions and issues? What about money matters? Is there an escrow representative who will provide information as to the status of escrow funds. How is the escrow arrangement handled?

In an ideal situation, the agency should present a team that will be the Intended Parents' team to positively and competently manage the surrogacy journey. Further, the agency team should be able to link up with the clinical team at the fertility center (the clinic) so that there is coordination among and between the agency team and the clinical team. The agency should know when the medical testing and protocol is to begin and should assist with travel arrangements, appointments, questions, logistics, communication issues and the like.

The agency will be instrumental in locating a gestational carrier in a State where it is favorable and legally feasible to embark on a successful surrogacy journey. The agency should coordinate the legal work and make sure that the legal issues are managed professionally and competently. If the gestational carrier is located in a different State from where the agency is located, the agency should be able to refer you to competent attorneys in the State where the gestational carrier resides. In this way, the legal issues in the birthplace will be addressed.

Surrogacy is not without risks but those risks can be minimized in numerous ways. For all of the above reasons, seek legal advice and consult surrogacy agency experts before taking on this journey. In so doing, you will be more likely to have an exciting and joyful experience in building your family.

3. Questions to Ask When Interviewing A Surrogacy Agency

1. How many years of experience do you have in matching surrogates with Intended Parents?
2. Approximately how many Intended Parents have retained your services in the past year? In the past three years?
3. Who are the team members that I would be working with?
4. What is the experience of the people on the team? What are their credentials?
5. Is there a lawyer on this team?
6. If not, who will be our lawyer for the

surrogacy contract?

7. How do you find or recruit your surrogates?

8. What is the screening process you use to make sure the surrogates are suitable for carrying a surrogate pregnancy?

9. Do you conduct a psychological evaluation prior to presenting the Carrier to us?

10. If not, do you do a preliminary psychological evaluation and what does that consist of?

11. Do you conduct a criminal background check on the candidates to become Gestational Carriers?

12. Does your agency obtain the potential Carrier's medical records and have them reviewed by a fertility physician in advance of proposing her as a Carrier?

13. If the potential Carrier is married, does the screening extend to her Husband?

14. How long does it take to find a Surrogate?

15. Are there any Surrogates or Gestational Carriers available now?

16. How do you propose the Gestational Carrier to us (me)?

17. Do you present a list of multiple Carriers from which I choose a Carrier?

18. Do you present one Carrier at a time?

19. What criteria do you use to propose a Carrier to me or to us? How do you determine who might be a suitable Carrier for us?

20. Who conducts the initial meeting between the Carrier and us?

21. What States do the Carriers come from?

22. Do the Gestational Carriers have insurance?

23. How are insurance issues handled?

24. If the Gestational Carrier does not have medical insurance, does your agency help us to procure medical insurance?

25. What are the options to obtain medical insurance for a Gestational Carrier?

26. What kind of a relationship will the Carrier want to have with us after the birth?

27. Do we have any obligations to keep up a relationship?

28. What kind of a relationship do Intended Parents usually have with their Carrier during the pregnancy?

29. Will we have access to her medical records for the pregnancy

30. Will we be able to be present at the birth?

31. Who communicates to the hospital that this is a surrogate pregnancy and that we are the parents?

32. Who makes sure that we get an accurate and correct birth certificate?

33. Have you ever had any cases where the Carrier wanted to keep the baby?

34. How much will all of this cost?

35. Do you have a list of expenses and fees?

36. What differentiates your agency from other surrogacy agencies?

4. Definitions and Terms

Anonymous Egg Donor :   A woman who
undergoes a protocol to donate her eggs
(gametes, ova, ovum) to another person or
couple (recipient) in order for the eggs to
be used to create embryos that will belong
to the recipient. The donor remains
anonymous to the recipient(s) and she is
identified by a donor number.

Anonymous Sperm Donor: A man who donates
his semen (sperm) to another person or
couple (recipient) in order for the sperm to
be used to create embryos that will belong
to the recipient(s). The sperm donor
remains anonymous to the recipient(s) and
he is identified by a donor number.

Assisted Reproduction: The use of medical
techniques, such as drug therapy, artificial

insemination, or in vitro fertilization, to enhance fertility.

Assisted Reproductive Technology: (ART) any procedure that involves manipulation of eggs or sperm to establish pregnancy in treatment of infertility, such as in vitro fertilization, embryo transfer, egg and sperm donation, gestational surrogacy

Assisted Reproduction Technology Law: Laws involving assisted reproductive technology treatment, and the legal issues surrounding such treatment such as contractual matters between egg donors or sperm donors and recipients; surrogacy contracts and legal parentage issues

Birth Mother: The woman who carries a pregnancy and gives birth to the child; in Gestational Surrogacy, the birth mother is not necessarily the legal mother

Blastocyst: A blastocyst is an embryo that consists of 200 to 300 cells and is ready for implantation

Carrier: The Gestational Carrier, also referred to as Gestational Surrogate and Surrogate

Egg Donor: A woman who agrees to undergo a protocol of medication to produce multiple eggs, and who then donates those eggs (gametes, ova) to recipient Intended Parents; the donor is not to have legal rights to the eggs or the resulting embryos or child if a child is born

Egg Donor Contract: The written agreement or document between the Egg Donor and the recipient Intended Parents

Genetic Parent(s): The Intended Parent who is genetically related to the child to be born

Genetic Mother: The Intended Mother who is genetically related to the child to be born, ie, the Intended Mother who uses her own egg to create the embryos that will be transferred to a surrogate in the hope of achieving a pregnancy and birth

Genetic Father: The Intended Father who is genetically related to the child to be born, ie, the Intended Father who uses his own sperm to create the embryos that will be transferred to a surrogate in the hope of achieving a pregnancy and birth

Gestational Carrier: A woman who carries a baby for the Intended Parent(s), ie, another couple or individual who shall become the legal parent(s) of the child to be born. A Gestational Carrier is NOT genetically related to the baby she is carrying. The pregnancy was achieved by the egg of the Intended Mother or an egg from an egg donor

Gestational Surrogacy Contract (Agreement):

The written agreement or contract between the Gestational Carrier and the Intended Parents. This Agreement should be drafted by a lawyer familiar with assisted reproduction law, and it should be reviewed by competent legal counsel on behalf of the Gestational Carrier

Gestational Surrogate: A woman who carries a baby for another the Intended Parent(s), ie, another couple or individual who shall become the legal parent(s) of the child to be born. A Gestational Carrier is NOT genetically related to the baby she is carrying. The pregnancy was achieved by the egg of the Intended Mother or an egg from an egg donor

IVF: In Vitro Fertilization, ie the process by which an egg is fertilized by sperm outside the body: in vitro.

Intended Mother: The woman, in surrogacy

arrangements, who is not carrying the baby but who is intended to become the legal mother of the baby to be born to the surrogate

Intended Father: The man, in surrogacy arrangements, who is intended to become the legal father of the baby to be born to the surrogate

Intended Parent(s): There are single Intended Parents and there are Intended Parents in couples, both married and unmarried, straight or gay. The Intended Parent or Intended Parents are the individuals or couples who are intending to take custody of the child being born to their Gestational Carrier. They are intending to become the legal parents. In some cases, they are genetically related to the child and in some cases they may not be genetically related. But whether or not there is a genetic connection to the child carried by the Gestational Carrier, the Intended Parent or Intended Parents are to become the legal and custodial parents.

Known Egg Donor: A woman who is known to the recipient Intended Parents and who goes through a medical protocol for egg retrieval and donates the retrieved eggs to recipient Intended Parents who then use the eggs to create embryos. Usually a known egg donor is a relative such as a sister of the Intended Mother.

Known Sperm Donor: A man who is known to the recipient Intended Parents and who donates his sperm to recipient Intended Parents who then use the sperm to create embryos. Usually a known sperm donor is a relative such as the brother of the Intended Father.

Matching Agency: A firm or agency (or surrogacy

program) that is retained for the purpose of finding a suitable Gestational Carrier, and for supervising and monitoring the surrogacy arrangement. Services, competency and skills vary widely from agency to agency.

Pre-Birth Order (PBO): A court order obtained prior to the birth of a child being carried by a Gestational Carrier that provides for the establishment of the Intended Parents' legal parentage, and to place the names of the Intended Parents on the child's birth certificate

Post-Birth Order (PBO): Similar to a pre-birth order except that this court order is obtained after the birth. May be applicable in the event of a premature birth or for other reasons.

Recipient: The individual or couple who receives donated gametes, ie, eggs or sperm

Second Parent Adoption (also referred to as Co-Parent Adoption or Stepparent Adoption): This is a legal proceeding by which the non-genetic Intended Parent of a child born to a Gestational Carrier may have to establish legal parentage, depending on the law of the State where the birth took place, and the law of the State where the Intended Parents reside.

Sperm Donor: A man who donates his sperm to another individual or couple so that the individual may use the sperm to create an embryo or to achieve a pregnancy. The donor is not to have legal rights to the embryos or the child born as a result of the utilized sperm.

Step-Parent Adoption: See Second Parent Adoption

Surrogacy Agency: See Matching Agency

Surrogacy Contract (Agreement): See Gestational Carrier Contract

Surrogacy Matching Agency: A firm, company or agency that recruits Gestational Carriers and matches them with Intended Parents

Surrogate Mother: Also known as Gestational Carrier or Surrogate, this is a woman who carries a baby and gives birth to a baby for a couple who are the Intended Parents or an individual who is the Intended parent. The term Surrogate Mother applies to the woman carrying the baby whether or not she is genetically related to the baby. In Traditional Surrogacy circumstances, the term Surrogate Mother is more commonly used. In Gestational Surrogacy, the terms Gestational Carrier or Gestational Surrogate are more commonly used.

5. The Gestational Carrier Agreement

The Gestational Carrier Agreement is also called the Surrogacy Agreement or Surrogacy Contract (also known as the Gestational Surrogacy Agreement or Contract). The word agreement and contract are interchangeable when speaking about this written document. For our purposes, we will refer to it as the "Agreement."

Once again the law of the State where the Agreement is supposedly being entered into is very important since there are some States that maintain laws providing that it is against policy or even against the law to enter into a Surrogacy Agreement. Therefore, if someone enters into such an Agreement in a State where it is disallowed, the Agreement will not be valid or binding. Furthermore, and even more importantly, if the baby being carried by a Gestational Carrier is born in a State where surrogacy is against the law or against public policy, then there are few legal protections available to Intended Parents should something go wrong with the contractual relationship between the Gestational Carrier and the Intended Parents.

Gestational Surrogacy is a delicate arrangement, a relationship building process with the goal of achieving a pregnancy and having a child born who will be put into the arms of his or her waiting and rightful parents, that is of course, the Intended Parents. This delicate or fragile arrangement may be strengthened and may be fortified with a strong foundation and with solid intentions and positive direction through the help of professionals who will ensure that legalities are followed, that the Gestational Agreement is drafted (or entered into) in a State where it may be enforced, that the child is born in a State where Gestational Surrogacy is looked upon favorably and where there are laws, policies and procedures to protect the Intended Parents.

Contract law is an intricate and complex body of law that governs how contracts are made, construed, interpreted, and enforced. Therefore, when we are seeking to make a Gestational Surrogacy Agreement, contract principles apply. The basic principles provide that contracts must contain some basic elements:

1. Names of the parties;
2. Date and Place of the Agreement;
3. Signatures;
4. Consideration, otherwise known as the "bargained for exchange."

Needless to say, the Gestational Carrier Agreement will contain many more provisions than these basic elements.

a. Essential Provisions

There are certain topics or issues that must

be covered in the Gestational Carrier Agreement. First of all, the medical providers should be identified. For example the IVF clinic or reproductive physician should be named. Also, the obstetrician that the Gestational Carrier wishes to use should be identified with a further provision that the Intended Parents will have the opportunity to approve of the chosen obstetrician.

State law must be determined and the Agreement should indicate what that law is and what specific procedures should be followed. All parties must agree to follow these procedural requirements. Some examples of procedural requirements are legal proceedings to validate the Agreement prior to the embryo transfer (Texas), or attendance at Court for the pre-birth order regarding legal parentage and names on birth certificate (Connecticut).

Compensation terms must be outlined and detailed. See the section below covering the issue of compensation terms.

Usually, the Agreement speaks to how many cycles will be attempted by the parties. The general provision is for the parties to agree to continue working together for three (3) cycles. Also, the number of embryos to be transferred at each transfer is addressed. Often, the number of embryos is limited to two or three with a further provision that the parties will follow the reproductive physician's advice regarding the number of embryos to be transferred based on the quality of the "blasts" (embryos) and how many days old they are.

The Intended Parents and the Gestational Carrier must agree on some crucial decision-making issues that may arise during a pregnancy. The parties must agree as to whether or not there will be a termination of the pregnancy in the event of a severe birth defect. Or if the Gestational Carrier has a triplet pregnancy, the parties must agree as to whether they will attempt to sustain the triplet pregnancy. If the Intended Parents have a thought that they would want the Carrier to undergo a selective reduction, then the parties must indicate in the Agreement that they agree to this procedure (if requested by the Intended Parents).

Example:

In a recent case, the parties all agreed ahead of time that in the event of a triplet pregnancy, there would be a selective reduction. The reproductive physician transferred only two embryos. Both embryos successfully turned into a pregnancy. However, one of the embryos divided naturally into identical twins thereby turning the pregnancy into a triplet pregnancy. Once this happened, the Gestational Carrier had second thoughts and did not want to undergo the selective reduction procedure. The Intended Parents were distraught as they were advised that the pregnancy would be very high risk due to the medical circumstances of the pregnancy. In this case, the agency (Worldwide Surrogacy Specialists, LLC) became involved and assisted the parties with their communication, and with advice that a high-risk obstetrician should be consulted and the advice of this physician should be followed.

Soon thereafter, the Gestational Carrier went for the consultation. The high-risk physician advised that the selective reduction procedure should be done, and the Gestational Carrier agreed to the procedure.

This is an example of why it is a good idea to have a surrogacy matching agency in place, one that will attend to these issues and assist the parties in working out resolutions.

Furthermore, all parties should be in agreement that whenever a medical issue arises, they will consult with the medical professionals and follow their advice and guidance. Especially in the case of a high-risk scenario such as the conception of triplets.

b. Compensation Terms

Whenever anyone enters into a contract, they can essentially create the terms they wish to negotiate as long as the purpose of the contract is legal, and as long as the terms are not unconscionable or grossly unreasonable. However, in a Gestational Surrogacy Agreement, there are some standards or customary provisions that are generally expected when the compensation terms are outlined and drafted. There are usual and customary concepts and terms that are covered, and there are important legal issues that must be addressed.

Further, in Gestational Carrier Agreements, there are outlines of when payments are made, installment schedules, and terms for the reimbursement of lost wages or child care expenses that the Gestational Carrier may incur.

Most Gestational Carriers and Intended Parents are able to go on-line to various websites and forums to ascertain what types of compensation in these Agreements are reasonable and anticipated. For example, generally, Gestational Carriers are compensated within a range of $20,000 to $30,000. First-time Carriers are closer to the $20,000.00 provision while experienced Carriers, ie, those Gestational Carriers that have been Carriers already, often receive compensation in the area closer to $30,000.

There are exceptions to these concepts. There are Carriers who are paid much more, perhaps by wealthy Intended Parents who are able to pay more and perhaps have greater expectations of a Carrier. For example, there are celebrity Intended Parents who must insist on privacy and who expect their Carriers to bear the risk of publicity or the burden of intrusion into their private lives in the event the news of the surrogacy arrangement is leaked to the media.

On the other hand, there are Gestational Carriers who will carry for Intended Parents for no compensation or very little compensation. For example, a sister may carry a baby for her sister who cannot carry a child. Or there may be other family or relative situations. There are also friends who carry for friends. And there are Gestational

Carriers who are willing to help an Intended Parent who has dealt with chronic illness or hardship, and who has financial hardship. These Carriers may agree to become Carriers for little or no compensation.

Most often, the base compensation for a Gestational Carrier is divided into ten equal installments. Payments begin after there is a positive pregnancy test, such as a beta test or confirmation of the fetal heartbeat. There are other payments that are often part of a Gestational Surrogacy Agreement. Some examples are:

1. A payment of $500, more or less, for undergoing the embryo transfer including successfully completing the pre-transfer protocol;

2. There may be additional payments when the Gestational Carrier undergoes invasive procedures such as amniocentesis, selective reduction, C-Section or other invasive

procedures;

3. In the unfortunate circumstance of a miscarriage or the diagnosis of a severe birth defect, there may be payments for a D & C procedure, or termination of pregnancy; As a general matter, should a miscarriage or termination of pregnancy occur, the payments to the Gestational Carrier under the contract will stop unless the parties agree to go forward with a continued monthly allowance as they progress toward another embryo transfer.

4. Travel expenses, maternity clothing, childcare, lost wages, insurance premiums, medical co-pays, legal fees, and other miscellaneous expenses are usually covered in the Agreement.

5. In addition, there may be a provision for lost wages for the Gestational Carrier's Husband in case he loses time from employment for purposes of the surrogacy

arrangement;

6. Regarding the Gestational Carrier's travel, she may request travel expenses for a companion so that she is able to come to the IVF clinic for testing and for the embryo transfer with her Husband, or with a friend or relative.

7. Often, in contracts, there is a provision for a monthly allowance of around $200.00 per month. This may take the place of reimbursements for co-pays, local travel and babysitting (excepts perhaps childcare if the Carrier is placed on bed rest), and other routine expenses such as vitamins, and other miscellaneous expenses that are set forth in the Agreement.

It is important to note that the parties must have legal counsel. These Agreements are serious and they cover a life-changing course of events. In order to stabilize and strengthen the relationships between the Gestational Carrier, her Husband if she is married, and the Intended Parents, a clear and unambiguous Agreement is of paramount importance.

Therefore, it is necessary that the parties retain competent legal counsel. Usually the lawyer for the Intended Parents drafts the contracts. Another lawyer is retained to review and advise the Gestational Carrier and her Husband. These lawyers pay attention to the legal issues, the law of the State where the birth will take place, the terminology and drafting of the Agreement, and the compensation terms.

Should any negotiations or revisions be necessary, the lawyers deal with these tasks and explain the matters to their respective clients. It is very helpful that the lawyers take care of these matters not only to ensure compliance with the law and legal and contractual necessities for the Agreement, but also to spare the relationship and communications between the parties from the discussion of financial and legal issues. It frees the parties to engage in a more social and friendly relationship as they look forward to and actually begin to experience the surrogacy journey.

c. Rights of the Intended Parents

The Agreement will provide that the Intended Parents are to become the custodial and legal parents of the child to be born to the Gestational Carrier. This is the intention of all parties from the outset. All agree that the Intended Parents are the rightful parents of the child. This intention and agreement must be memorialized in the Agreement.

The Agreement will state who the Intended and legal parents are of the child. It will also indicate how the embryos were created. If the embryos were created from the egg and sperm of the Intended Mother and the Intended Father, the Agreement will state this and will indicate that the Intended Parents are also the genetic parents.

In the event an egg donor is utilized to create the embryos, the Agreement will provide for this so that all parties are aware of how the embryos are created, and all parties agree to these procedures and acknowledge in writing that they have been informed of the details of the making of the embryos. With proper signed documentation, the Egg Donor will have no rights to a child born of embryos created using the Egg Donor's eggs.

Whether or not the Intended Parents are genetically related to the embryos should not matter in terms of their right to become the parents of the child to be born. For example, under Connecticut law, as long as the Intended Parents and the Gestational Carrier are parties to a valid gestational carrier agreement, and as long as the case is one of gestational surrogacy, and a physician provides an affidavit detailing how the conception occurred, then, prior to the birth, the Intended Parents may be named as the legal parents of the child to be born, and their names will be placed on the child's birth certificate.

These Pre-Birth Orders (PBOs) may be obtained in other States as well but again, the parties must have competent legal counsel familiar with the State law and legal procedures.

D. Rights of the Gestational Carrier

When I argued the landmark surrogacy case of *Raftopol v. Ramey* before the Supreme Court for the State of Connecticut, I argued that Intended Parents should be granted parental rights prior to the birth of the child. One of the concerns of Chief Justice Chase Rogers was the extent of the rights that the Gestational Carrier does have. After all, she is giving of herself and her physical well-being to carry a child for someone else.

The Court was assured that the Gestational Carrier does have contractual rights by way of the Gestational Carrier Agreement. And, more importantly, the Gestational Carrier has the absolute right to make decisions regarding herself and the pregnancy by way of her constitutional right of privacy. See, *Roe v. Wade,* 410 U.S. 113 (1973), the landmark Supreme Court case holding that the Due Process Clause of the United States Constitution protects the right to privacy, including a woman's right to terminate her pregnancy, against State action to try to control this right.

It should be noted too that there may be cases in the reverse, where the Gestational Carrier decides that she does not wish to terminate the pregnancy although the Intended Parents have notified her that they are requesting the pregnancy be terminated. Again, the Gestational Carrier does have the right to make that decision, however, under the contract, the Intended Parents may be entitled to claim that the Gestational Carrier is in breach of her contractual obligations and, therefore, no longer entitled to compensation or other benefits under the contract.

In this situation, another question arises. If the Gestational Carrier decides to sustain a pregnancy that the Intended Parents wish to terminate, do the Intended Parents have an obligation to take custody of the child. This may seem to some like an unnecessary inquiry, however the question has come up in certain arrangements. The likely answer is that the Intended Parents must take responsibility for the child and must assume custody.

E. Notes Re: Gestational Surrogacy Contracts

Surrogacy is an arrangement of fragile

relationships and risks. The relationships are
made stronger with the help of competent
professionals such as the physicians, lawyers and
psychologists who engage with the parties to
assure that issues are addressed, discussed and
resolved during all phases of the surrogacy
journey. The process will never be risk-free but
again, the risks may be minimized with the
assistance of a knowledgeable and competent
professional team who can assess the risks and
guide the parties into a fully negotiated and
understood Gestational Surrogacy Agreement, and
further guide the parties through the process of
medical treatment, embryo transfer, pregnancy,
court proceedings, and birth.

The Intended Parents may now be asking
themselves, what about our rights to insist that the
Gestational Carrier carry the pregnancy to term,
take care of herself, avoid cigarettes and alcohol,
or recreational drugs for that matter. And what
about the rights of the Intended Parents to request

a termination of pregnancy in the case of a severe birth defect, or to decide on a selective reduction if there is a multiple pregnancy that is deemed high-risk?

This is where the contractual obligations and intentions as stated in the Gestational Surrogacy Agreement play an important role. Presumably, the Gestational Carrier will have little or no incentive to refuse to follow the wishes of the Intended Parents since that would potentially place her in a breach of contract situation and may be a reason for the Intended Parents to cease paying the compensation due under the terms of the Agreement.

Further, this emphasizes the importance of the matching criteria, i.e., the question as to whether or not a Gestational Carrier is the right match for the specified Intended Parents. Issues such as events that may require a termination of pregnancy, or that may cause serious consideration of selective reduction should have been discussed and agreed to before there was a pregnancy, Again, a competent surrogacy agency or a knowledgeable attorney working in the field of assisted reproduction technology law will have addressed such issues during the contract drafting and negotiations leading to the execution of the final Agreement.

F. Medical Decisions

The above sections regarding Agreements and contractual rights have covered some of the issues regarding medical decisions. However, there are still some issues that should be addressed.

One important provision for a strong surrogacy arrangement is that the parties agree to medical providers, including the reproductive endocrinologist (the infertility physician), and the obstetrician. Further if the pregnancy becomes a high-risk pregnancy, the parties should agree on a high-risk obstetrician.

The reason such agreement is essential is because when it comes time to make medical decisions, it will be important for all parties to pay close attention to the physicians' advice and recommendations. Obviously, if there is agreement on these doctors, then there will be a common goal or consensus to follow the advice of the chosen doctors.

Also, the Agreement or Contract should speak to the issue of decision-making. Even though the Gestational Carrier has the right to make decisions concerning her body and physical well-being, she is agreeing in the Contract that it is her intention to follow the decisions of the Intended Parents when it comes to the pregnancy. Examples include when the Intended Parents request genetic testing or when the Intended Parents request that the Gestational Carrier take medication or refrain from taking medication.

Other issues include the question of how
many embryos to transfer. This decision is made in
close consultation with the reproductive physician
and the embryologist as they determine the age
and quality of the embryos, also called blastocysts.

Once there is a pregnancy, other matters
for decision-making may arise: as considered
earlier, if there is a pregnancy with a serious birth
defect, will the Intended Parents wish to
terminate the pregnancy? If the Gestational
Carrier conceives triplets, what will the Intended
Parents wish to do, consider maintaining the
pregnancy or consider selective reduction? If the
pregnancy is high-risk, selective reduction may be
a very necessary and serious consideration for the
health of the carrier and the pregnancy.

The Intended Parents must work closely
with their agency and they should get to know
their Gestational Carrier so that these issues, if
they arise, may be solved in a positive and

synergistic manner.

6. Conclusion

Simply put, it is essential to have a competent team of medical and legal professionals in place for a successful surrogacy journey. The endeavor should be one of excitement and hope. Of course there will be tension and nervousness, and details that may at times seem overwhelming. But if the right team is on your side, you will be able to call on your team to answer questions and sort out details and to assist in the process each step of the way.

This primer on Gestational Surrogacy is authored by Attorney Victoria T. Ferrara, Legal Director and Owner of Worldwide Surrogacy Specialists, LLC, 2150 Post Road, Fairfield, CT 06824. 203.255.9877.
www.assistedreproductionlaw.com

For more information on the Worldwide Surrogacy program, email Attorney Ferrara at vferrara@victoriaferrara.com

Made in the USA
Charleston, SC
11 November 2015